SOUS VIDE

COOKBOOK

FOR

EVERYONE

*The Ultimate Guide for Beginners on
How to Cook Like a Chef at Home*

Kara Ashton

Table of Content

Introduction

Sous vide is a French term meaning "under vacuum". It describes a cooking technique in whichthe vacuum-sealing food in a bag is submerged into the water bath and kept at an accurate temperature for a certain period of time. For this process we use a tool called immersion circulator. This method maintains the taste, texture, nutrients and smell of food. You may be surprisedhow many delicious recipes you can make in a water bath.

Three simple steps of this cooking method:

- Connect the sous vide machine to the pot of water and adjust the cooking temperature
- Now, place your food in the sealable bag and remove the air from it
- Now, put the bag in pre-heated water and cook for as long as you need. If the bag is floating you can clip it to the side of the pot, just to be sure that the food will be cooked evenly.

If you want to get a more crispy food, you can still grill or fryit. Thanks to sous vide technique, you can eat and cook healthy and crispy food which maintain your good health.

Pro Tip:
The more fresh the ingredients, the better your food tastes. You should use good quality, unprocessed ingredients for these recipes. Don't forget thatby using flavorful ingredients, you get incredible results.

The benefits of Sous Vide:

Tasty food —delicious and very juicy food, because you don't have to marinate the food for a long time before but you will cook it in the marinade and the food's juices. Thanks to that it's moist and very tender.

Consistency — You can cook your favorite food at a constant temperature and amount of time, without really doing anything more. It doesn't require from you neither more skills nor more attention.

Less waste —food usually loses its volume because of drying out. It doesn't happen to food cooked with this technique so you waste less.

What you need to start with sous vide?

- Sous Vide circulator
- Sous Vide containers
- Ziplock bags
- Searing tools (optional)

About recipes:

I wrote 100 different flavorful sous vide recipes and with pleasure shared it in my cookbook. You can find here all types of meals for lunch, dinner, breakfast, dessert and so on. Choose your favorite sous vide recipe and cook some delicious steaks, vegetables, and other dishes. If you prefer to have more crispy food then go ahead and sear it after you have finished cooking it with sous vide. You can pan fry it as it's the easiest method and you surely already have at home a pan and a stove.

You will love it!

Healthy Chicken Caprese

Serving: 2
Preparation Time: 10 minutes
Cooking Time: 2 hours

Ingredients:

For the chicken:
- Two chicken breasts – boneless, skinless
- Half teaspoon kosher salt
- Half teaspoon garlic powder
- Half teaspoon onion powder
- Half teaspoon dried basil
- Half teaspoon dried oregano
- Five cracks fresh black pepper
- One tablespoon olive oil
- Two tablespoons balsamic vinegar
- Six fresh basil leaves

For the caprese topping:

- One cup quartered cherry tomatoes
- One tablespoon olive oil
- 1/4 teaspoon kosher salt
- Two cracks fresh pepper
- One small garlic clove minced
- Three fresh basil leaves
- Two ounces fresh mozzarella pearls
- Balsamic glaze – drizzling

Instructions:

For the chicken:

- First, prepare the sous to vide water to 170 degrees F. Place the chicken breast into sous-vide bags.
- In the little bowl, whisk the onion powder, dried oregano, salt, onion powder, olive oil, balsamic vinegar, pepper, dried basil, and garlic powder until combined well.
- Pour half marinade into all bags and massage marinade into the chicken until combined well. Add three basil leaves into all bags.
- Seal the bags and then place them into the hot water bath for two hours.

For the Caprese topping:

- When cooking time completes, take out water bath with tongs, keep it aside and make the topping.

- Place mozzarella, olive oil, tomatoes, basil, garlic, pepper, salt, and stir to combine into the little bowl.
- Open the bags and place chicken on the serving platter. Top with tomato mixture and drizzle balsamic vinegar and serve!

Chicken Caesar Salad

Servings: 2
Preparation Time: 5 minutes
Total Time: 5 minutes

Ingredients:

- Two sous vide chicken breasts
- One head romaine lettuce – rinsed and chopped
- caesar dressing
- Grated parmesan cheese
- Croutons

Instructions:

- First, grill the sous vide chicken breast for one minute and dice on the cutting board.
- Toss the dressing with diced sous vide chicken breast, croutons, lettuce, and parmesan cheese in the medium bowl.

Tasty Mashed Potatoes

Servings: 6
Preparation Time: 5 minutes
Cooking Time: 50 minutes

Ingredients

- Two pounds Gold potatoes
- 4 oz. unsalted butter
- Half cup heavy cream
- Half cup milk
- 1 1/2 tsp. Diamond kosher salt
- Freshly ground pepper

Instructions:

- First, preheat the water bath to 194 degrees F.
- Dice and peel the potatoes into 1" slices.
- Add all ingredients to the bag and use the water displacement method to remove the air and close.
- Perform the quick squeeze test until cooked well.

- Transfer the potatoes to the bowl and mash them.
- Drain the liquid into a hot bowl and then pass the cooked potatoes through a food mill and stir to combine.
- Serve warm.

Delicious Duck Breasts

Servings: 2
Preparation Time: 5 minutes
Cooking Time: 2 hours 5 minutes

Ingredients:

- Two duck breasts
- Olive oil
- Kosher salt & freshly ground pepper

Instructions:

- First, preheat the water to 130 degrees F.
- Score the fat side of the breast with a knife but be careful not to pierce the meat.
- Drizzle with olive oil and season the breast on both sides.

- Place in the Ziplock bag and water displacement method to remove the air and close the bag.
- Cook in the water bath for one and half hours to three hours.
- Remove the bag from the water bath and place it on the counter to chill five minutes before dissolving in the ice bath.
- Remove the breast from the bag and dry with a paper towel.
- Preheat a skillet over medium to high flame and then put the duck breast for five minutes until crisp.
- Turn over the breast and remove the skillet from the flame.
- Cook for half-minute and then add on the cutting board.

Let rest for five minutes before slicing and sprinkle with salt.

Sous Vide Carrots

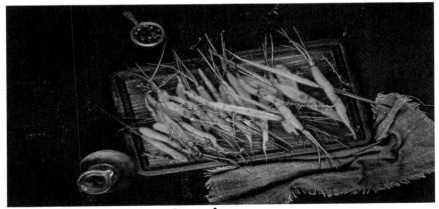

Servings: 4
Preparation Time: 5 minutes
Cooking Time: 1 hour

Ingredients:

- One bunch carrots – washed, peeled or scrubbed
- Kosher salt & freshly ground pepper
- Six sprigs fresh thyme
- Two Tbsp. unsalted butter

Instructions:

- First, preheat the sous vide water to 185 degrees F.
- Place the carrots into the Ziplock bag with thyme, kosher salt, butter, and pepper, and then seal the bag.

Sous vide for forty-five minutes to one hour until carrots get soft and serve

Sous Vide Polenta

Servings: 4
Preparation Time: 5 minutes
Cooking Time: 2 hours

Ingredients:
- One cup coarse cornmeal
- Two cups water
- Two cups whole milk
- One tsp. Diamond kosher salt
- Four Tbsp. unsalted butter
- Half cup grated Parmigiano-Reggiano cheese
- One Tbsp. chopped fresh herbs such as thyme, rosemary, chives

Instructions:
- First, preheat the water bath to 185 degrees F.
- Mix the butter, cornmeal, salt, milk, and water in the Ziplock bag.

- Squeeze the ingredients, especially the butter.
- Add in the water bath and use the water displacement method to remove the air. Seal the bag and cook for two hours.
- Now, remove the bag from the water bath and move it to the serving bowl.
- Combine in fresh herbs and Parmesan cheese and serve warm!

Best Turkey Breast

Preparation Time: 15 minutes
Cooking Time: 3 hours
Total Time: 3 hours 15 minutes

Ingredients:

- 2 to 4 pound turkey breast
- Two tsp. Diamond kosher salt
- Freshly ground black pepper
- Two Tbsp. neutral oil such as canola or vegetable

Herb Marinade

- Three Tbsp. unsalted butter
- One tsp. fresh rosemary – chopped
- One tsp. fresh thyme – chopped
- Four sage leaves – chopped

Instructions:

- Preheat the water bath to 145 degrees F.

For seasoning:
- Add herbs and butter to the hot skillet until brown. Please move to the ramekin and keep it aside to cool, not to melt the plastic bag.
- Season the turkey breast with freshly ground and kosher salt.
- Place the seasoned breast in the Ziplock bag, pour the butter seasoning, and then use the water displacement method to remove the air from the zip lock bag.
- Cook in the water bath for three to four hours.
- Remove from the water and sit on the counter in the bag for fifteen minutes to cool before searing.
- But be careful not to overcook.
- Remove the breast from the sealed bag and dry with a paper towel.
- Now, sear the breast with a broiler or skillet, or grill.
- Use two tbsp of oil to coat the base of the pan and cook over a high flame.
- Sear the dried turkey breast on the skin side for one minute until brown and then flip.
- Sear on the other side for one minute.
- Slice and serve!

Yummy Crème Brûlée

Servings: 6
Preparation Time: 10 minutes
Cooking Time: 1 hour
Cool Time: 25 minutes

Ingredients:

- Five egg yolks
- 1/3 cup granulated sugar
- 1/4 tsp. Diamond kosher salt
- Two cups heavy cream
- One tsp. vanilla extract
- Turbinado sugar

Instructions:

- Whisk the salt, vanilla, egg yolks, heavy cream, and granulated sugar in the bowl until dissolved for half-minute.

- Strain the custard base through a strainer into a big cup.
- Pour into Mason jars without overfilling past the thread line.
- Set the water bath to 178 degrees F.
- Place the lids on the pot but do not over tighten and then add to the water bath using tongs.
- When water is at temperature and cooks for one hour.
- Remove the jar from the water bath, place it on the baking dish with ice, and cool for 25 to 30 minutes.

To Finish the CremeBrulee:
- Sprinkle the thin layer of turbinado sugar on the top of the custard.
- Caramelized the sugar let it cool for a few minutes before serving.

Healthy Scrambled Eggs

Servings: 2
Preparation Time: 1 minute
Cooking Time: 15 minutes
Total Time: 16 minutes

Ingredients:

- Three large fresh cold eggs
- Two tablespoons whole milk
- One tablespoon melted butter
- Optional: fresh thyme, chopped bacon
- Kosher salt & freshly ground pepper

Instructions:

- First, preheat the sous vide water bath to 167 degrees F.
- Whisk the milk, melted butter, and eggs in the bowl and then pour into the Ziplock bag.

- Place in the water bath and use the water displacement method to seal the bag.
- Cook for 16 to 17 minutes and remove every five minutes to massage with hands.
- Remove from the pack and season with pepper and salt, and serve!

Sous Vide Eggs

Servings: 1
Cooking Time: 13 minutes
Total Time: 13 minutes

Ingredients

- Large fresh cold eggs
- Kosher salt & freshly ground pepper – serving

Instructions:

- First, preheat the sous vide water bath to 167 degrees F.
- Set the eggs at the base of the container using a slotted spoon.
- Cook for thirteen minutes and half minutes and then run under cold water for half a minute or into an ice bath for few seconds until cool.
- Crack and move this into the bowls and season with pepper and kosher salt.

Sous Vide Pork Shoulder

Servings: 10
Preparation Time: 10 minutes
Cooking Time: 22 hours

Ingredients

- 4 to 5 lb Boneless Pork Shoulder or Boston Butt – trimmed

Dry Rub

- 1/8 cup Smoked Paprika
- Two tbsp Kosher Salt
- Two tbsp Packed Dark Brown Sugar
- Half tbsp Granulated Sugar
- One tbsp Dark Chili Powder
- One tbsp Ground Cumin
- Half tbsp Dried Oregano
- Half tbsp Ground Black Pepper

- Half tbsp Celery Seeds

Instructions:

- Set the sous-vide water bath to 165 degrees F in the container until wholly submerged.
- Now, trim additional fat from the pork shoulder.
- Make a dry rub by mixing all dry rub ingredients in the bowl or spice shaker.
- Directly rub over the pork.
- Place the pork shoulder in the sealed bag and then close.
- Place the vacuum-packed pork shoulder in the sous vide water bath and cover for eighteen hours to one day.
- Remove from the water bath and place it in the freezer.

Tasty Pork Tenderloin

Servings: 4
Preparation Time: 5 minutes
Cooking Time: 1 hour 32 minutes

Ingredients:

- One whole 1 to 1 1/2 point pork tenderloin
- Kosher salt & freshly ground black pepper
- Fresh thyme and rosemary sprigs
- Canola oil - searing
- Butter – basting

Instructions:

- First, fill the big pot with hot water and heat the water bath to 139 degrees F.
- Season the pork with freshly ground pepper and kosher salt, and then add in the Zip lock seal bag with rosemary sprigs and a little thyme.

- Use the water displacement method to seal the bag and remove the air from the pack. Please place it in the water before sealing.
- Now, cut the bag to the container's side to keep it dissolved and cook for one and a half hours to four hours.
- Remove from the water bath and remove the pork from the bag and dry with a paper towel.
- Now, heat heavy-bottom skillet over high flame and drizzle in canola oil to coat the base and sear for half-minute to brown on each side.
- Let sit for a few minutes before slicing!

Herb Crusted Leg of Lamb

Preparation Time: 15 minutes
Cooking Time: 3 hours 30 minutes
Total Time: 11 hours 45 minutes

Ingredients

For the Lamb Leg
- 1 4 to 6 pound bone-in Lamb leg - trimmed
- 1/3 cup kosher salt
- Freshly ground black pepper
- 1/4 cup fresh rosemary leaves
- 1/4 cup fresh thyme leaves
- Half teaspoon crushed red pepper flakes
- Zest from one lemon
- Half cup extra virgin olive oil

For the Italian Salsa Verde
- Two coarsely chopped garlic cloves
- Half teaspoon kosher salt
- 1/4 teaspoon crushed red pepper flakes

- Lemon zest
- Two tablespoons lemon juice
- Half cup extra virgin olive oil
- One cup coarsely chopped Italian parsley
- One tablespoon capers – rinsed and drained
- Two chopped anchovy filets

Instructions:

- Make herb marinade: mix the thyme, olive oil, rosemary leaves, lemon zest, and red pepper flakes in the food processor and pulse until chopped.
- Dry the lamb with a paper towel and sprinkle the fresh ground pepper and salt over the lamb legs and rub the herb mixture all over the lamb.
- Place the lamb leg in the Ziplock bag and seal it and place it in the freezer overnight.
- Let sit the lamb for some time before cooking.
- Set the sous vide temperature to 133 degrees F and cook the lamb for three to five minutes.
- When lamb leg cooked, preheat the broiler.
- Remove the lamb leg from the bag, move to the sheet pan, and dry with a paper towel.
- Rub with olive oil and place under the broiler until browned, for four to five minutes.
- Place the lamb leg on the cutting board and then slice,
- Serve with Verde sauce and sprinkle with sea salt.

Make Italian salsa verde:

- Add all ingredients to the blender and pulse until smooth. Season and add more lemon juice and salt.
- Place in the container and cover with the wrapper.
- Please place it in the freezer.

Sous Vide Pot Roast

Serving: 6
Preparation time: 15 minutes
Cooking time: 24 hours
Total time: 24 hours 15 minutes

Ingredients:

- Two Pound Chuck Roast
- ¼ Cup Lemon Juice
- ¼ Cup Soy Sauce
- One teaspoon Minced Garlic
- One Sprig Fresh Rosemary

Instructions:

- Combine the garlic, lemon juice, rosemary, and soy sauce.
- Place the roast inside and rub in the marinade.
- Seal the bag and remove the air.

- Place in the sous vide cooker to 130 to 140 degrees F.
- Cook for eighteen hours to one day.
- Now, take out the bag and turn the roast in the marinade.
- Heat olive oil in the big saucepan.
- Sear the roast for one minute.
- Serve!

Garlic Herb Butter Steaks

Preparation Time: 10 minutes
Cooking Time: 1 hour
Total Time: 1 hour 15 minutes

Ingredients:

- Two pounds Filet Mignon 4 1/4 pound steaks
- Two teaspoons kosher salt
- One teaspoon black pepper
- 1/4 teaspoon garlic powder
- Two tablespoons butter
- One clove garlic finely minced
- Two tablespoons parsley flat leaf
- One tablespoon vegetable oil

Instructions:

- Season the steaks with pepper, garlic powder, and pepper.
- Now, heat sous vide to medium-rare temperature.
- Heat the water bath to 130 degrees F and set the timer for one hour.
- When water gets hot, submerge the steaks in the bag and seal.
- When steaks are cooking, prepare garlic butter and mix the softened butter with parsley, minced garlic, and a pinch of salt.
- Remove the steaks from the water bath after 1 hour.
- Heat the cast-iron skillet over a high flame and add one tablespoon olive oil.
- When the oil is smoking, sear the steaks for a half minute to one minute.
- Top with butter and let rest, and serve!

Special Grasshopper Cheesecake

Preparation Time: 15 minutes
Cooking Time: 1 hour
Additional Time: 4 hours
Total Time: 5 hours 15 minutes
Serving: 6

Ingredients:

- Two large chocolate graham crackers
- Two tablespoons butter melted
- 1 8 ounce block of cream cheese – softened
- Half cup sugar
- Three eggs
- Half teaspoon mint extract
- Two drops green food coloring
- 1/4 cup cream
- Half cup chocolate chips

- Andes Candy chocolates

Instructions:

- Make the chocolate crust:
- Melt the two tablespoons butter in the microwave-safe bowl.
- During this, grind the chocolate graham cracker.
- Mix the chocolate cracker crumbs and melted butter.
- Add one tablespoon of chocolate graham crack crust of six jars and press into the base to make the crust.

Sous vide grasshopper cheesecakes:

- Set the sous vide to 176 degrees F and add chocolate graham cracker crust in every jar.
- Add the grasshopper cheesecake batter into the pot.
- Place the lid and tighten a ring on to every jar.
- Now, lower into the sous vide bath and set the timer for 1 hour.
- When cook, remove the pot from the tub and store it in the freezer until ready to serve!
- Add chopped Andes chocolate as garnish.

Eggs with Avocado Toast

Servings:4
Preparation time: 10 minutes
Cooking time: 45 minutes
Total time: 55 minutes

Ingredients

- Four whole Eggs
- Four slices Ciabatta Bread or Thick Cut Bread
- Four tablespoons Butter
- One whole Avocado – pitted and skin removed
- Half whole Lemon – juiced and zested
- Sea Salt – seasoning
- McCormick Sriracha Seasoning – garnish
- Queso Fresco – crumbled for garnish
- Arugula Micro Greens

Instruction:

- First, preheat the cooker to 147 degrees F. Lower the eggs into the water bath and cook for forty-five minutes.
- Remove to the paper towel-lined plate using a slotted spoon.
- Spread butter on each slice of bread and use extra butter on the bread.
- Heat the big pan over a medium-high flame, and then add extra butter and bread. Toast until golden brown on every side, for two minutes.
- Remove to the serving platter and scatter avocado slices on the toast.
- Squeeze lemon juice and zest over to the top.
- Sprinkle with sea salt.
- Crack the egg on the paper towel and move sous vide egg with a spatula to every toast.
- Season with sriracha and sprinkle with crumbled queso and garnish with microgreens and serve!

Sous Vide Filet Mignon

Serving: 1
Cooking Time: 1 hour
Total Time: 1 hour

Ingredients

- 4 1- inch thick filet mignons
- Two Tablespoons butter
- One Tablespoon olive oil
- Kosher salt & pepper

Instructions:

- Set the sous vide to 132 degrees F.
- Seal the filet mignons.
- Cook for one hour.
- Remove steak and dry with a paper towel – season with pepper and salt.

- Preheat a cast-iron skillet over a high flame. Add butter and oil and sear for one minute per side.
- Spoon butter over them and serve!

Buffalo Chicken Lettuce Wrap

Serving: 4
Preparation time: 10 minutes
Cooking time: 1 hour 15 minutes

Ingredients:

For chicken:
- One cup buffalo sauce
- One tbsp honey
- One tbsp chili lime Cholula
- Three garlic clove – minced
- Three lbs chicken breast
- Half lime juice
- One tsp green scotch bonnet pepper sauce
- One tbsp butter
- Pepper and salt

For wraps:

- Shredded carrots
- Celery – sliced
- Blue cheese or ranch dressing
- Gorgonzola cheese
- Six lettuce leaves

Instructions:

- Set the sous vide cooker to 150 degrees F.
- Trim and season chicken with pepper and salt and place in the zip lock bag.
- Whisk honey, green scotch bonnet pepper sauce, half cup buffalo sauce, chili lime Cholula, and garlic. Add sauce over the chicken.
- Now, use the water immersion method to seal the bag, place it in the water bath, and set it for one hour.
- Remove the chicken from the zip lock bag and store the liquid. Cut the chicken into pieces using two forks.
- Melt one tbsp butter in the saucepan and then add the liquid from the half cup buffalo sauce, half lime, reserve cooking liquid, and boil.
- Add the chicken and boil the sauce and stir to coat.
- Place half cup shredded buffalo chicken into leaf for lettuce wraps.
- Top with carrots, gorgonzola, and celery.

Chicken Breast with Lemon

Serving: 4
Preparation time: 5 minutes
Cooking time: 2 hours
Additional time: 5 minutes
Total time: 2 hours 10 minutes

Ingredients

Sous vide chicken breast

- Two chicken breast - bone
- Half lemon
- Two sprigs rosemary
- Two sprigs thyme
- salt and pepper
- One Tablespoon oil or butter
- One teaspoon capers

Instructions:

- Set sous vide cooker with water bath at 145 degrees F.
- Season chicken breast with pepper and salt. Place chicken breast in the zip lock bag with thyme, two slices of lemon, and rosemary.
- Add all ingredients to the sealed bag.
- When the sous vide cooker has reached 145 degrees F and add chicken to the water bath and cook for one and a half hour to four hours.
- When chicken gets to cook, heat the cast iron pan over medium to high flame. Add the tablespoon butter or oil.
- Take out the chicken from the bag and add herbs and lemon. Dry with a paper towel.
- Brown the chicken in the skillet for one minute until brown on the top.
- Let chicken rest for five minutes until cool.
- Peel the chicken from breast bone using the thumb.
- Slice the chicken and serve with capers, lemons, and herbs!

Mustard and Molasses Pork Belly Strips

Servings: 4
Preparation Time: 10 minutes
Cooking Time: 4 hours
Total Time: 8 hours 10 minutes

Ingredients:

- 500 Grams Pork Belly Strips
- 1/4 Cup Molasses
- 1/4 Cup Dijon Mustard
- 1/4 Cup Apple Cider Vinegar
- One Teaspoon Black Pepper
- Salt

Instructions:

- Combine the vinegar, black pepper, mustard, and molasses in the bowl.

- Marinate pork belly overnight.
- Add pork with the marinade in a sous vide bag.
- Cook for four hours at 170 degrees F.
- Season with salt.

Tasty Steak & Potatoes

Servings: 4 to 6
Preparation time: 3 and half hours
Cooking time: 15 minutes

Ingredients

- 2 12-ounce strip steaks
- Six garlic cloves
- Two sprigs of rosemary
- Six sprigs of thyme
- One pound baby potatoes
- Six baby carrots
- Ten stalks of asparagus
- Four peeled Cipollini onions
- One ounce of unsalted butter
- Kosher salt and fresh cracked pepper

Instructions:

- First, preheat the sous vide in a big pot of water to 125.6 degrees F.
- Season two strips of steaks with pepper and salt and add in the zip lock bag with rosemary, garlic, and thyme, and remove air before sealing it. Keep it aside.
- Take a separate bag; add in the asparagus, butter, potatoes, onion, pepper, carrots, salt, and remove the air before sealing it.
- Place the bag into a water pot, cook for forty-five minutes, and add in steak and cook for an additional one hour.
- Remove the steak from the bag and place on the fire-safe station, and sear until golden brown until internal temperature achieved.
- Slice the steak and serve!

Lamb Chops with Basil Chimichurri

Serving: 4 to 6
Preparation time: 10 minutes
Cooking time: 2 hours 10 minutes

Ingredients:

Lamb chop:
- Two rack of lamb – frenched
- Two cloves garlic – crushed
- Pepper
- Salt

Basil Chimichurri:
- One cup fresh basil – chopped
- One to two cup garlic clove – minced
- One tsp red chili flakes
- One shallot diced
- Three tbsp red wine vinegar

- ¼ tsp sea salt
- ¼ tsp pepper
- Half olive oil

Instructions:

- Set the sous vide temperature to 132.8 degrees F – season with pepper and salt.
- Seal lamb with garlic and sous vide for two hours.
- Mix all basil chimichurri sauce ingredients in the bowl and combine well – season and cover with a lid.
- Please place it in the freezer to generate the flavor.
- After two hours, remove lamb chops from the bag and dry with a paper towel and sear with a torch.
- Slice and top with basil chimichurri sauce.

Healthy Corned Beef and Cabbage

Serving: 6 to 8
Total Time: 48 Hours

Ingredients:

- Four pounds of corned beef
- Six slices of bacon
- One head of cabbage
- Two cups chicken stock
- Half cup champagne vinegar

Instructions:

- First, preheat the water oven to 134 degrees F.
- Add the corned beef into the vacuum sealing bag.
- Submerge the pouch in the water oven and cook for forty-eight hours.
- Prepare the cabbage for forty-five minutes.

- Cook the bacon pieces over medium flame in the skillet until crisp and rendered.
- Pour one to two tablespoons of bacon fat.
- Add cabbage strips to the skillet and increase the flame and cook for five minutes.
- Add the vinegar and chicken stock to the pan and cook the cabbage in the liquid until tender.
- When cabbage gets tender, remove the corned beef from the water bath and cooking pouch.
- Slice the corned beef!

Tasty Kalbi Short Ribs

Servings: 4
Preparation time: 5 minutes

Ingredients:

- Sixteen crosscut beef short ribs
- Two cups cooked rice
- Kimchi

For the marinade

- Two tablespoons sesame oil
- Two tablespoons brown sugar
- 1 ½ teaspoons chili flakes
- One tablespoon chopped garlic
- Half cup soy sauce
- ¼ cup chopped green onions
- ¼ cup orange juice

Instructions:

- Boil the garlic in sesame oil in the pan for two minutes over medium to high flame.
- Add remaining ingredients and stir to make a marinade.
- Place beef ribs into the baking pan, pour the marinade over them and marinate for one hour and cover with the lid.
- Place in the freezer and flipping the ribs every fifteen minutes.
- During this, fill and preheat the sous vide water oven to 138 degrees F.
- Remove the ribs from the marinade and shake well.
- Place the ribs into four cooking pouches and vacuum seal on a moist setting.
- Submerge the pouches in the water oven and cook for three hours.
- During this, place the marinade into a pan and boil and cook for fifteen to twenty minutes until reduced.
- When ribs cook well, remove from the water bath and brush with reduced marinade.
- Finish the ribs on a grill pan for two minutes until caramelized. Serve with kimchi and rice!

Wagyu Beef Meatballs

Servings: 12
Preparation time: 20 minutes
Cooking time: up to 4 hours

Ingredients:

- 1 pound Wagyu ground beef
- ¼ cup dried bread crumbs
- 2 to 3 ounces milk
- Half teaspoon salt
- ¼ teaspoon black pepper
- One large egg – beaten
- Half shallots – peeled, diced
- Three tablespoons fresh parsley – chopped
- One tablespoon dried oregano
- One tablespoon garlic powder
- Three tablespoons grated Parmesan cheese

For serving:

- Barbecue sauce – for cocktail meatballs
- Marinara or Putanesca sauce

For searing:
- 1 to 2 tablespoons high-smoke-point oil

Instructions:

- Combine ground meat with all ingredients in the bowl until combined but do not over mix.
- Make the mixture into balls. Place the meatballs onto the tray, freeze them for 1 or 2 hours and then add them into the vacuum sealing.
- Fill and preheat the sous vide water oven to 135 degrees F.
- Submerge the pouch to cook for one hour for little meatballs and three to four hours for big meatballs.
- Remove the meatballs from the pouch and serve with sauce.

Wagyu Beef Brisket

Serving: 6 to 8
Preparation time: 20 minutes
Cooking time: 48 hours

Ingredients:

- 3 to 4 pounds Lone Mountain Wagyu (or other beef) brisket
- Dry rub
- One to Two tablespoons butter
- One sprig rosemary

For the dry rub
- Three tablespoons granulated sugar
- Two tablespoons brown sugar
- Two teaspoons garlic powder
- 1 1/2 teaspoons chili powder
- 1 ½ teaspoons paprika

- 1 ½ teaspoons cumin
- One teaspoon salt
- One teaspoon onion powder
- Two teaspoons ground black pepper

Instructions:

- Fill and preheat the sous vide water oven to 132 degrees F.
- Combine all rub ingredients in the bowl and combine well.
- Cut into pieces and season the brisket on both sides with rub and add into the vacuum seal.
- Submerge in the water oven to cook for forty-five hours.
- Heat the skillet over a high flame until hot.
- Remove the brisket and dry with a paper towel and sear in the skillet on one side for one minute.
- Turn to sear the other side and add the rosemary and butter to the skillet.
- Baste the meat in foaming butter for one minute.
- Slice and serve with favorites

Sous Vide Bacon

Serving: 4
Cooking time: 7 minutes
Total time: up to 2 days

Ingredients:

- One pound thick-cut bacon – 450 g

Instructions:

- First, preheat sous vide water to 145 degrees F.
- Place bacon in the water bath and cook for up 48 hours.
- When ready to serve, remove from the water bath and cool in the freezer.
- Preheat a big skillet over medium to high flame for five minutes.
- Add bacon and cook, pressing with the back of a spatula until brown and crisp, for two minutes.

- Turn bacon and cook on the other side and remove the pale color for fifteen seconds.
- Add on the paper towel-lined plate to remove the fat and serve!

Spicy Teriyaki Skirt Salad

Servings: 4
CookingTime: 4 hours 30 minutes

Ingredients:

For The Steak
- 1 1/2 pounds skirt steak
- Kosher salt and freshly ground black pepper

For The Dressing
- One tablespoon sesame oil
- One small yellow onion chopped
- Half cup soy sauce
- Half cup mirin sweet Japanese rice wine
- Half cup sake
- Half cup granulated sugar
- Five slices of peeled ginger
- Two cloves of garlic smashed

- One heaping tablespoon tobanjan
- One teaspoon finely grated garlic
- One tablespoon corn starch
- One teaspoon toasted sesame seeds

For The Salad
- One pound spring greens
- One cup shredded carrot
- One cup shredded daikon
- Three scallions white parts only – julienned

Instructions:

For The Steak:
- First, pepper and salt the steaks, Sear in a cast-iron skillet over forty-five seconds on each side.
- Place the steaks in a Ziplock bag in a single layer.
- Use the displacement method and place into a water bath 130 degrees F for four hours.
- Remove the steaks from the water bath and add them to the counter, and reserve any juices.

For the dressing:
- Heat the sesame oil in the pot over medium flame and cook onion until softened for five minutes.
- Add steak juices, soy sauce, garlic, mirin sake, and sugar, ginger to the pot and boil, and then cook for fifteen minutes.
- Sieve through a strainer and remove solids.
- Add back the sauce to medium flame and then add tobanjan and grated garlic.

- Combine water and one tbsp cornstarch in the little bowl until the milky texture and then add this to the pot and cook until thickened for three minutes.
- Remove from the flame and combine in sesame seeds, and corn starch

Icy Mango Basil Popsicle

Serving: 4
Preparation time: 10 minutes
Cooking time: 10 minutes

Ingredients:

- 1 Ib frozen mango chunks
- 1/3 C sugar
- four basil leaves
- two tsp fresh ginger – minced
- 1 C coconut milk – coconut cream

Instructions:

- Set circulator to 181. 4 degrees F.
- Whisk the sugar and coconut milk in the saucepan and continue whisk over medium flame until mixture begins to boil.
- Remove from the flame and cool in the freezer.

- Place the basil leaves, minced ginger, mango chunks in a big sous-vide pouch, and add coconut milk.
- Seal and cook for 1 hour.
- After cooking, cool thoroughly and open the pouch and remove the basil leaves.
- Combine well until smooth and then add into ice pop molds.
- Freezer for 4 hours or overnight and then serve

Icy Popsicle with Melon

Serving: 8
Preparation time: 20 minutes
Cooking time: 30 minutes

Ingredients:

- Honey dew melon
- ¼ C honey
- ¼ C fresh lime zest
- Half C sugar

Instructions:

- Set the circulator to 181.4 degrees F.
- Rinse and trim melon and then slice in half.
- Remove the inner membrane and seeds and then dice melon flesh into little cubes.
- Mix the honey, sugar, diced melon, and lime zest in the bowl and combine well. Transfer to the sous vide bag or pouch and seal.

- Cook in the water bath for a half-hour.
- After cooking, add liquid into Popsicle molds and freeze for three hours or overnight.

Mocha Pot de Crème

Serving: 8
Preparation time: 15 minutes
Cooking time: 30 minutes

Ingredients:

- ½ C espresso
- ¾ C milk
- 1 C heavy cream
- 6 egg yolks
- 1/3 C sugar
- 6oz chocolate – chopped
- Whipped cream – garnish
- Cinnamon powder – garnish

Instructions:

- Heat the espresso, heavy cream, and milk in the saucepan over medium to high flame.

- When boiling, remove the saucepan from the flame and stir in chocolate and stir well until smooth for fifteen minutes to cool.
- Mix the sugar, egg yolks, and salt in the medium bowl. Stir and slowly incorporated the chocolate crème mixture and whisk until smooth.
- Keep it aside to cool for an additional 10 to 15 minutes.
- Add all contents in the sous vide bag or pouch and close it.
- Cook at 180 degrees F for a half-hour.
- After cooking, remove from the pouch and add in the bowl and whisk unto ramekins and cool for at least 2 hours or until firm.
- Garnish with cinnamon powder or whipped cream.

Sous Vide Citrus Yogurt

Preparation Time: 15 minutes
Cooking Time: 3 hours
Total Time: 6 hours 15 minutes

Ingredients:

- 1 liter full-cream milk
- half cup yogurt
- half tbsp orange zest
- Half tbsp lemon zest
- Half tbsp lime zest

Instructions:

- Heat the milk at 180 degrees F on the stove top. Cool down to 110 degrees F over the bowl of ice and stir in yogurt

- Fold in the citrus zest and add into the canning jars, and place lid.
- Cook for three hours at 113 degrees F.

Sweet Plums with Red Wine Granita

Servings: 4
Preparation Time: 10 minutes
Cooking Time: 30 minutes
Total Time: 1 hour 10 minutes

Ingredients:

- Half cup sugar
- One cup red wine
- Four pieces plums

Instructions:

- First, cut the plums in half and discard stones.
- Heat the sugar and red wine in the saucepan until the sugar gets dissolve.
- Place plums in sous vide bag with sugar mixture and red wine.

- Cook for half hour at 170 degrees F.
- Freeze the poaching liquid and serve with granite!

Blueberry and Saffron CremeBrulee

Servings: 5
Preparation Time: 15 minutes
Cooking Time: 1 hour
Total Time: 2 hours 15 minutes

Ingredients:

- ¼ cup brown sugar
- two cups heavy cream
- four egg yolks
- Pinch saffron threads

Instructions:

- First, heat the saffron threads and cream in the saucepan.
- Whisk the sugar and egg yolks in the bowl.
- Now, temper the heated cream into the egg yolks.
- Strain the custard mix through a strainer.

- Add blueberries into the jars and add custard into the jars.
- Place lid on the jars.
- Cook at 176 degrees F for one hour.
- Let cool on the counter for a half-hour to one hour.
- Please place it in the freezer for four hours.
- Now, take out of the freezer and sprinkle sugar on the top.

Black Pepper and Mint Pineapples

Servings: 4 people
Preparation Time: 10 minutes
Cooking Time: 1 hour
Total Time: 2 hours 10 minutes

Ingredients

- One Pieces Pineapple – peeled
- 1/3 Cup Brown Sugar
- 1 Teaspoon Black Peppercorns
- Pinch Salt
- Handful Mint Leaves

Instructions:

- Cut and peel the pineapples into quarters.
- Combine the mint, brown sugar, salt, mint leaves, and black peppercorns in the mortar and pestle.

- Now, rube the pineapple wedges with sugar mixture and place them in a sous vide bag.
- Cook for at least one hour at 170 degrees F.

Ginger Tea Pears with Jelly

Servings: 2 people
Preparation Time: 10 minutes
Cooking Time: 2 hours
Total Time: 4 hours 10 minutes

Ingredients

- Two Pieces Pears peeled
- One Cup Water
- Half Cup White Sugar
- Two Tablespoons Ginger – thinly sliced
- Three Stalks Lemongrasses bruised
- 6 to 8 Pods Green Cardamom
- Five Pieces Star Anise
- One Tablespoon Black Peppercorns
- Half Tablespoon Unflavored Gelatin Powder

Instructions:

- Mix the cardamom, water, black peppercorns, sugar, lemongrass, star anise, ginger in the saucepot and boil for 5 minutes and strain through a strainer and cool.
- Now, peel the pears and add them to the sous vide bag with spiced ginger syrup.
- Add in a water bath and preheat to 189 degrees F for 2 hours.
- Dissolve the cooked pears into an ice bath.
- Move poaching liquid into the saucepot. Add gelatin and boil.
- Add gelatin into the mold and place it in the freezer until set.
- Serve pears with light syrup and jelly.

Sweet Vanilla Lemongrass Syrup

Servings: 1 cup
Preparation Time: 10 minutes
Cooking Time: 2 hours
Total Time: 4 hours 10 minutes

Ingredients:

- Two Cups Brown Sugar
- 1/4 Cup Water
- One Pod Vanilla
- Stalks Lemongrass

Instructions:

- Rub the lemongrass stalk with the blunt edge of a knife and wrap it into a bundle.
- Now, combine the vanilla, water, lemongrass, and sugar, in the sous vide bag.

- Cook for two hours at 194 degrees F. Cool in an ice bath.
- Strain through a strainer and serve!

Tasty Mango-Coffee Preserve

Preparation Time: 5 minutes
Cooking Time: 30 minutes
Total Time: 1 hour 5 minutes

Ingredients:

- Two Pieces Ripe Mango – diced
- Three Cups Brown Sugar
- One Piece Lemon juice and pith
- Two Tsp Instant Coffee

Instructions:

- Toss the sugar, instant coffee, mangoes, and lemon in the bowl.
- Spoon the mixture with lemon into canning jars, place the lid on and cook for a half-hour at 194 degrees F.
- Please put it in the freezer before serving.

Sous Vide Sweet Flan

Servings: 8
Preparation time: 10 minutes
Cooking time: 1 hour 5 minutes
Additional time: 20 minutes

Ingredients:

- ¾ cup white sugar
- 8 4-ounce Mason jars with lids and rings
- 14 ounce sweetened condensed milk
- 12 fluid ounce evaporated milk
- Three eggs
- One tablespoon vanilla extract

Instructions:

- Place sous vide cooker inner side big heat-proof containers fill with water—preheat the water bath to 179 degrees F.
- Melt the sugar in a saucepan over medium flame until browned, for five minutes.
- Add melted sugar into 8 Mason jars and cover the bottom of each.
- Combine the evaporated milk, vanilla extract, condensed milk, and eggs in a separate bowl, add to the pots, and close.
- Place jars in the water bath and adjust the time to one hour on a timer.
- Remove the jars from the water bath and let cool the flan for twenty minutes.
- Uncover the pot and stir with a little spatula and serve!

Delicious Peach Cobbler

Serving: 2 to 3
Preparation time: 15 minutes
Cooking time: 3 hours

Ingredients

- 4 ounces self-rising flour
- 7 ounces granulated sugar
- One cup whole milk
- One teaspoon vanilla extract
- Eight tablespoons unsalted butter – melted
- 2 cups peaches – chopped

Instructions:

- Set the sous vide cooker to 195 degrees F and grease canning jars with non-stick oil spray or butter.

- Whisk the sugar and flour in the big bowl and whisk in vanilla and milk until smooth. Stir peaches and butter.
- Split the batter between the jars. Smear sides and tops of jars using a towel. Seal the pot on the counter to remove air bubbles.
- Place lid and seal until tight, put in the water bath, and set the timer for three hours.
- When time finishes, remove the jars from the water bath and place them on the cooling rack. Remove the lids of the jars. Let cool for ten minutes before serving.

Chocolate Pot De Crème

Servings: 8
Preparation time: 30 minutes
Cooking time: 1 hour

Ingredients:

- Two bars Green & Black's Salted Caramel Dark Chocolate
- Two cups heavy whipping cream
- Seven egg yolks
- Half cup sugar
- Half teaspoon salt

Instructions:

- Adjust the sous vide cooker to 162 degrees F.
- Combine the dark chocolate and heavy cream in the little saucepan and heat over medium flame

until the chocolate gets melted and whisk until combined well.

- Remove from the flame and keep it aside.
- Take a separate bowl; add egg yolks to it and add salt and sugar to the egg yolks and whisk.
- Add egg yolk mixture to the chocolate cream mixture and whisk until incorporated. Spoon the mixture into jars.
- Lowe the jars into the bath with a spoon and cook for one and a half hours.
- Remove and place it in the freezer for six hours or overnight.
- Serve with berries and whipped cream.

Vanilla Bean Ice Cream

Servings: 10
Preparation time: 20 minutes
Cooking time: 1 hour

Ingredients:

- One cup whole milk
- One cup heavy cream
- Half cup granulated sugar
- Six large egg yolks
- One teaspoon vanilla bean paste
- Pinch kosher salt

Instructions:

- Set the sous vide cooker to 180 degrees F.
- Add all ingredients to the blender and puree until frothy and smooth, for half-minute.

- Please move to the zip lock bag and seal it using the water immersion method.
- Put in the water bath and set the timing for one hour.
- Agitate the pack many times to prevent clumps.
- When the timer finishes, remove the bag from the water bath and place it in the ice bath to cool.
- Churn the mixture in the ice cream, make until set and freeze and serve!

Yummy Vanilla Pudding

Servings: 6
Preparation time: 15 minutes
Cooking time: 45 minutes

Ingredients:

- One cup whole milk
- One cup heavy cream
- Half cup ultrafine sugar
- Three large eggs
- Three tablespoons cornstarch
- One tablespoon pure vanilla extract
- Pinch kosher salt

Instructions:

- Set the sous cooker to 180 degrees F. add all ingredients in the blender and puree until frothy and smooth, for half-minute.
- Add to the zip lock bag, seal it using the water immersion method, put it in the water bath, and set the timer for forty-five minutes.
- Agitate the bag many times to prevent clumps.
- When time finishes, remove the bag from the water bag and then add the contents of bag to the blender and combine until smooth.
- Add in the bowl and place it in the freezer and serve!

Coconut Rice Pudding

Servings: 2
Preparation time: 10 minutes
Cooking time: 4 hours

Ingredients:

- Two cups whole milk
- 14-ounce unsweetened coconut milk
- Half cup arborio rice
- Half cup granulated sugar
- Half cup coarsely shredded unsweetened coconut
- One teaspoon ground cinnamon
- Half teaspoon ground ginger
- Half teaspoon kosher salt

Instructions:

- Set the sous cooker to 180 degrees F.

- Add all ingredients to the zip lock bag. Seal the bag and place it in the water bath, and set the timer for four hours.
- When time completes, remove the bag from the water bath.
- Please place it in the freezer for up to 2 days.

Boneless Beef Short Rib

Servings: 4
Preparation time: 30 minutes
Cooking time: 48 minutes

Ingredients:

- 2 lb boneless beef short ribs
- Kosher salt and freshly ground black pepper
- 1 tbsp olive oil

Instruction:

- Set the sous vide cooker to 130 degrees F. Season the beef with pepper and salt.
- Heat the oil in the big skillet over a high flame until smoking.
- Sear the beef until golden brown and keep it aside and cool for ten minutes.

- Seal beef in the bag and cook for 4 hours.
- Remove the ribs from the bag and let sit for ten minutes.
- Slice the grain and serve!

Red Curry Crusted Beef Prime Rib

Servings: 2 Steaks
Preparation Time: 15 minutes
Cooking Time: 40 minutes
Total Time: 1 hour 35 minutes

Ingredients

For the Steaks
- two Pieces Beef Prime Rib Steaks
- two Tablespoons Thai Red Curry Paste
- Salt – taste

For the Raita
- 1.5 Cups Cucumber – deseeded and thinly sliced
- One Cup Red Radish – thinly sliced
- Onr Piece Red Thai Chili – finely chopped
- Bunch Fresh Basil chiffonade
- Bunch Fresh Mint – chopped

- Two Cloves garlic – finely chopped
- One Tablespoon Honey
- One Tablespoon Fish Sauce
- One Tablespoon Tamarind Paste

Instructions:

- Combine chili, honey, garlic, basil, tamarind paste, fish sauce, and mint in the bowl.
- Toss radish and cucumber and cover and chill until serve.
- Season steaks with salt, add in sous vide bag and cooks for forty minutes at 130 degrees F.
- Now, place steaks in the ice bath.
- Brush steaks with red curry paste on all sides.
- Sear steaks for forty-five seconds in the cast-iron pan.
- Let rest for ten minutes and serve with cucumber raita.

Healthy Greek Burger

Servings: 2
Preparation Time: 15 minutes
Cooking Time: 45 minutes
Total Time: 1 hour 40 minutes

Ingredients

For the Patties
- 500 Grams 80/20 Ground Beef
- One Tablespoon Dried Marjoram
- One Tablespoon Dried Oregano
- One Tablespoons Dried Parsley Flakes
- One Tablespoon Salt
- Half Tablespoon Black Pepper

For the Feta Cream
- 2/3 Cup Heavy Cream
- Half Cup Feta Cheese crumbled
- Half Tablespoon Garlic Powder
- One Teaspoon Black Pepper

- Half Teaspoon Salt

For Serving
- Two Pieces Burger Buns
- One Piece Red Onion – thinly sliced
- Fresh Parsley – chopped
- Lettuce

Instructions:

- Make 8oz patties and season with dried herbs, salt, and pepper.
- Add the patties into the sous vide bags—Cook for forty minutes at 140 degrees F.
- During this, make the feta cream and whisk the cream and egg yolks in the saucepan over a low flame until thickened.
- Crease in the garlic powder, pepper, feta cheese, and salt.
- Move the patties to the ice bath; Sear the patties in the cast iron for one minute. Top with red onion slices, feta cream, fresh parsley, and lettuce.

Beef Kaldereta

Servings: 6
Preparation Time: 8 hours
Cooking Time: 1 day
Total Time: 2 days 8 hours

Ingredients

- One Kilogram Beef Short Ribs
- One Piece Red Onion cut into chunks
- One Piece red bell pepper diced
- One Large Carrot cubed
- Half Cup Green Olives
- One Cup Tomato Sauce
- half Cup Liver Pate
- Two Tablespoons Worcestershire Sauce
- Salt
- Pepper

Instructions:

- Marinate the beef in black pepper and Worcestershire overnight and season with salt and sear in a warm pan and keep it aside.
- Cook the carrots, onions, bell pepper, olives; Stir in tomato sauce and liver pate.
- Place the sauce and beef into sous vide bag and cook for one day at 150 degrees F.

Beef Shogayaki

Servings: 4
Preparation Time: 5 minutes
Cooking Time: 12 hours
Total Time: 1 day 5 minutes

Ingredients

- 500 Grams Beef Stew Meat
- Three Tablespoons Soy Sauce
- Three Tablespoons Mirin
- Three Tablespoons Water
- One Thumb-Sized Piece Ginger grated

Instructions:

- First, mix the mirin, ginger, soy sauce, and water.
- Toss the beef in the soy-ginger mixture.
- Transfer the marinade and beef to the sous vide bag.

- Cook at 140 degrees F for twelve hours.
- Drain the beef out of cooking juice and sear for one minute in the hot pan.

Chicken Tikka Masala

Servings: 4
Preparation Time: 15 minutes
Cooking Time: 1 hour
Total Time: 2 hours 15 minutes

Ingredients

- 500 Grams Chicken Breast Fillet cubed
- One thumb-sized piece Ginger – finely chopped
- Six Cloves garlic finely chopped
- One Piece Red Onion finely chopped
- Half Cup Diced Tomatoes
- Three Tablespoons Garam Masala
- One Cup Coconut Milk
- Handful Fresh Cilantro chopped
- 1 to 2 Tablespoons Ghee
- Salt – taste

Instructions:

- Cook the onions, garlic, and ginger in the ghee or oil until the onion gets translucent.
- Add the diced tomatoes and cook for an additional one minute.
- Add garam masala and cook for an additional minute.
- Add coconut cream and season with salt and stir and turn off the heat.
- Puree the sauce in the blender, add the sauce and chicken into the sous vide bag, and cook for one hour at 145 degrees F.
- Top with fresh cilantro

CPSIA information can be obtained
at www.ICGtesting.com
Printed in the USA
BVHW062138300321
603712BV00006B/663

9 788396 082749